I0021500

Snooze. Pin. ~~Done.~~

Getting Things Done with Inbox by Gmail

A detailed examination into Google's latest groundbreaking entry into email management.

Special Bonus Section
Inbox Zero in 3 Simple Steps Using Inbox by Gmail

Written by
Scott Greenstone, Google Top Contributor, Gmail
& Inbox by Gmail

Layout by
Russ Buchmann, Google Top Contributor, Gmail
& Inbox by Gmail

About the Authors

Scott Greenstone is a self-proclaimed Google Fan Boy. His love of all things Google brought him to Inbox by Gmail and eventually to the Google Product Forums where he quickly rose within the ranks to Top Contributor. Since becoming involved with the Google Product Forums and the Top Contributor Program *(http://www.google.com/get/topcontributor/)*, Scott has become a Top Contributor in Gmail, Inbox by Gmail, Project Fi, Google Calendar, and Google Play. He is a Registered Nurse and works full-time in electronic medical record implementation. Scott lives with his wife, two children, and dog on the East Coast of the United States.

Russ Buchmann is a tech enthusiast (geek) who enjoys following the latest trends in technology and gadgets. He has been a long time user of many Google products and services and finds great satisfaction in helping other people learn about new things that can make their lives better, more productive or just more fun. Russ is also a Top Contributor for Gmail and Inbox by Gmail as well as a Rising Star in Google Photos. For his day job, he is the head of IT for a regional retail chain and dabbles in marketing, design, and photography. He and his wife are the proud parents of two boys and share their home with three cats.

Acknowledgements

We can never claim to have learned all that we have learned about Gmail and Inbox by Gmail without the help of the incredible team of Rising Stars and Top Contributors as well as our Community Managers Andres Bravo, Crystal Coleman and Jordan Esparza. We can never thank them enough for all of their help and knowledge sharing.

Introduction

On April 1, 2004, Google announced something so revolutionary and so groundbreaking that everyone believed it was in fact an April Fool's joke. However, the world was surprised when this announcement turned out to be real. As a response to people complaining about the lack of quality in existing email services and programs, Google introduced Gmail to the world.

But Gmail was not going to be just another email program. Gmail was going to be fast and efficient. Users would also be able to keep their email forever with the 1gb of free storage. When Google introduced Gmail back in 2004, it was somewhat of an exclusive club. One that required users to obtain an invitation that was not necessarily easy to come by. A little over a year later, Gmail introduced the ability for current users to invite their friends to use the service.

Fast forward 10 years, and Gmail now offers 15gb of free storage to over 1,000,000,000 accounts. Yes, that number does seem astonishing. There are more than ONE BILLION Gmail accounts worldwide.

Email has really changed dramatically in the past 30+ years. Not only do we receive more email, but we also handle and use email differently. Email has become our repository for important information, our task list, our portal for calendar invites, as well as our primary means of conducting personal and professional business.

What does a company that changed the landscape of email do after 10 years of tremendous growth and success? Reinvent the wheel again, of course. So, following the same invitation only model of its predecessor, on October 22, 2014, Inbox by Gmail was introduced to the world. Inbox by Gmail was touted as "an inbox that works for you"[1], and it most certainly has lived up to that promise.

~~Inbox helps bring simplicity t~~o these activities with Bundles, Assists,

[1] http://gmailblog.blogspot.com/2014/10/an-inbox-that-works-for-you.html

Snooze, and Reminders. These new features, coupled with many of the existing features in Gmail and a simplified user interface on both web and mobile, have won over millions of users. As of this writing, between 10,000,000 and 50,000,000 copies of Inbox by Gmail have been downloaded from the Google Play store alone.[2]

This book has been written with the intention of being the most complete guide to all that Inbox by Gmail can do. The following pages include descriptions, pictures, and tips on how to get the most out of Inbox by Gmail. And as a special bonus, I have included one of my most Plus 1'd and viewed posts: Inbox Zero in 3 Simple Steps.

It must be mentioned that at the time of this writing, as far as I am aware, there are no intentions of Google shutting down the original classic Gmail program.

---

[2] https://play.google.com/store/apps/details?id=com.google.android.apps.inbox

Table of Contents

Inbox by Gmail: The Basics

Inbox is not just a new interface for accessing your Gmail. It's an entirely new way to manage your email. It's a minimalistic, highly graphical display of your messages that provides important information up front. This allows users to quickly manage messages in order to reach the oh-so-coveted Inbox Zero.

Icons and what they mean

With the introduction of Inbox and its new thoughts on handling email came some new icons that rarely have been seen before in email programs. These new icons control how you and Inbox handle your emails. Essentially, there are four icons that determine what happens with an email in Inbox. These icons include the Pin (🖈), Snooze (🕓), Done (✔), and Sweep (✅). Each of these will be described later in much more detail

Composition

Composing in Inbox is as simple as using the red circle with a plus sign ⊕, known as the FAB (Floating Action Button). Hovering over this button on the web (or single tapping on mobile) will display a speed dial of sorts that provide the options for creating reminders or emailing directly to one of the three most frequent people with which you have contact. Clicking on this button on the web, or tapping twice on mobile, will just open a new blank compose screen without any recipients populated.

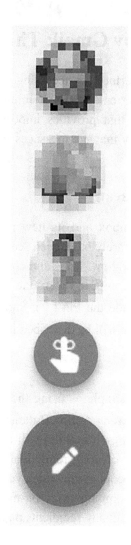

Once in the compose screen, you have some basic formatting options. Your options include bold, italics, underline, bullets, numbering, links and the standard attachment options. To add recipients to the "To:", "CC:", and "Bcc:" fields, simply click on the down arrow to the right of the "To:" field. You can even select what account you want to send the email from if you have any "Send As" accounts setup. You can learn more about "Send As" accounts by going to *http://goo.gl/X4oIOq*.

SEND 📎 **B** *I* <u>U</u> <u>A</u> ▾ T̞T ▾ Sans serif ▾ ☰ ☷ 🔗 ✕

Attachments

Adding attachments is definitely an important feature for any email program. In order to attach files using Inbox, simply click on the paperclip icon in the compose window. On the web, you will be presented with a slide out showing your recently attached files, Google Drive, and Google Photos access, as well as the option to access the file manager of the system you are using.

For some file types, when you initially attach a file it will show the entire image as an inline image. However, Inbox will give you an option to change this to send as an attachment as opposed to an inline image. This is accomplished by clicking on the three vertical dots on the top right of the image and choosing "Send As Attachment". This too can be reversed by hovering over the thumbnail of the attachment and clicking on the three vertical dots again to select "Send Inline". The three vertical dot menu also provides the user with the ability to remove the attachment as well.

Attaching files from Google Drive will only give you the option to add as an in-line file, not as an attachment. In addition, as when sharing anything from Google Drive, you will be presented with the share permissions dialogue based on the current sharing permissions of the item you are sharing.

Saving Attachments

Receiving attachments is a little different in Inbox than most other email programs. When an email arrives in Inbox that has an attachment, you will have a small highlight to show that there is an attachment. (Highlights will be covered later in this book). This makes accessing the attachment much easier so you do not have to dig through many emails in a conversation to find which one has the attachment. Attachments will be listed in the order in which they are received from left to right so you will know which is the most recent in the event of multiple iterations of a file. Once in the preview screen, you will have options for printing, downloading or adding the attachment to your Google Drive.

If the attachment is in a Google Doc format and you are using chrome with the Google Docs/Sheets/Slides extension installed, clicking on the file will open it in the appropriate Google application, Docs, Sheets, Slides, etc. Other file types will open in a preview window that will give you an option to download the file unless you have a specific extension that enables native viewing of the file. In addition, when previewing a file, you have the option to save the file directly to Google Drive.

Printing Messages

Printing options in Inbox are limited. Simply put, you can only print the current message and not the entire thread or discussion. Just click the three vertical dots to the right of Sender and choose Print. This will bring up the standard print dialogue box where you will have print options and output options such as which printer or if you want to print to PDF.

Replying and Forwarding

Responding to messages in Inbox is as simple as can be. Essentially, you have three options: Reply All, Reply to Sender, or Forward.

To reply to all recipients in an open email, click in the reply area below the message where it says "reply to all" and start typing. This is somewhat of a default action.

If you just want to reply to the sender, click on the single arrow pointing to the left ↖ on the right side of the reply box. To pop-out the email into a separate box after selecting the reply method you want, just click the pop out reply icon ⮰.

To forward an email, click on the single arrow pointing to the right ➡. This will automatically provide you with a pop-out reply window.

In order to change what action you are already taking, just click on the red word Draft or the pop-out reply icon ⮰. This will give you a menu to change your action. This menu will also provide options to edit the recipients or the subject. Choosing to edit recipient or subject will automatically provide you with the pop-out reply.

Whether you are replying in-line or using the pop-out window, you will have a toolbar with full rich text formatting options.

For many emails, you may notice some suggested replies. This is a great machine-learning feature that has been incorporated into Inbox to help save you time. You can learn more about this feature below in the "Mobile" chapter under "Smart Replies".

Inbox Bundles: These Ain't Your Ordinary Grocery Bundles

Bundles are Inbox's new take on email organization. Similar in nature to the classic Gmail labels, Inbox helps you keep all of your emails packaged together nicely under a common heading. There are two types of bundles in Inbox: System Generated and User Generated. Both of these types of bundles can be further divided into two categories: Bundled in the Inbox and Unbundled. I know, that sounds a bit confusing. How can you have a bundle yet call it unbundled? More on that a bit later.

System Generated Bundles

System generated bundles are exactly what they sound like. They are created by Inbox to help organize common emails that all users receive. These bundles cannot be renamed or deleted, however they can be configured to only show up in your Inbox on a certain schedule. System generated bundles have nice, colorful icons to help you quickly identify them. There are 9 system generated bundles, 8 of which are shown to the left. The 8th bundle is the Trips Bundle, which will be discussed separately a little later, and the 9th bundle is the Saved bundle, also discussed later in this book.

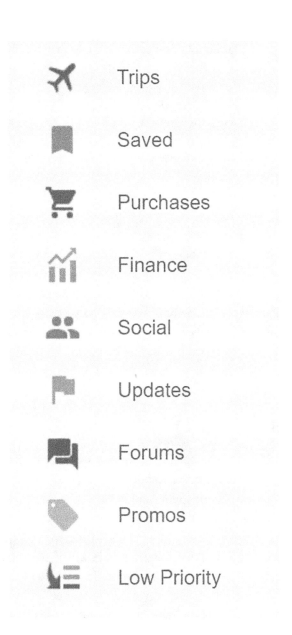

Trips

Saved

Purchases

Finance

Social

Updates

Forums

Promos

Low Priority

Emails you receive are automatically categorized on the back end because, as the Inbox team says, "some messages just belong together"[3]. But, as with all Google products, you don't have to agree with how Google

---

[3] http://www.google.com/inbox/

categorized a particular email. You can move one or more messages out of a particular bundle, add them to a bundle, or remove the bundling all together for a particular message or group of messages.

A brief summary of each system bundle would be helpful at this point.[4]

1. **Purchases:** your purchase confirmations, receipts, and shipping emails
2. **Finance:** your bills, bank statements, and credit card statements
3. **Social:** your messages from Twitter, G+, and other social media sites
4. **Updates:** your messages from any online accounts you may have
5. **Forums:** your mailing list and discussion group messages
6. **Promos:** your deals, offers and marketing emails
7. **Low Priority:** These are messages that you are less likely to be interested in. However, most of these messages are found in other system bundles as well. It should be noted that this bundle is only enabled by default if you used Priority Inbox or Important First Inbox in classic Gmail.

Trips Bundle

When we go on trips, whether for business or pleasure, there are usually multiple emails that are received about that trip. We receive reservation confirmations for car, hotel, flight, and activities, as well as the multitude of reminder emails and status updates. Inbox provides an incredible feature that literally bundles all of the related messages together into one convenient package. The Trips bundle places all of the related messages for a trip together in what I call a sub-bundle. Essentially, it is a bundle within a bundle. These trips are conveniently named and include a cover photo of the destination. All of this is done automatically for you on the backend.

---

[4] https://support.google.com/inbox/answer/6050237?hl=en&ref_topic=6067574

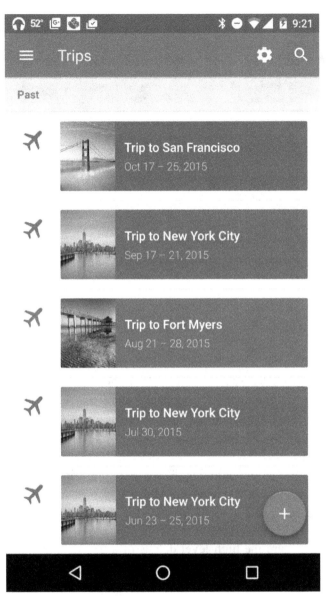

Once you open up the bundle you will see a quick summary of your flights and any relevant information in between such as car rental, hotel, and activities. These are easily identified by icons related to the data. Below the summary information, you have all of the related emails listed so you can see any additional information without having to dig for it.

You are also provided with the ability to add emails to a trip or remove emails from a trip.

On travel day, your Trips Bundle will appear in your Inbox. As you get travel related updates such as flight status and travel status, your Trips Bundle will be automatically updated such as on-time, delayed, or cancelled. As the Inbox team has said "Inbox is smart enough to only show you the most up-to-date information.[5]"

Inbox also allows you to add emails to an existing trip in the Trips Bundle for the times when a message couldn't be parsed automatically or the algorithms were unable to recognize it as trip related.

You can also share the high level details of a trip with another via email. This will send an email to the other user with a "smart mail" card of formatted plain text to display in their email program regardless of whether they use Inbox by Gmail or not.

---

[5] http://gmailblog.blogspot.com/2015/06/trip-bundles-in-inbox-by-gmail.html

Newsletter Bundles

Newsletter Bundles essentially create a magazine rack for you in Inbox for each newsletter you receive. For newsletters that currently have this functionality, a heading card will be created and top stories will be highlighted at the top and new stories will indicated by bold headings. If you expand the bundle, a full history of earlier content will be displayed.

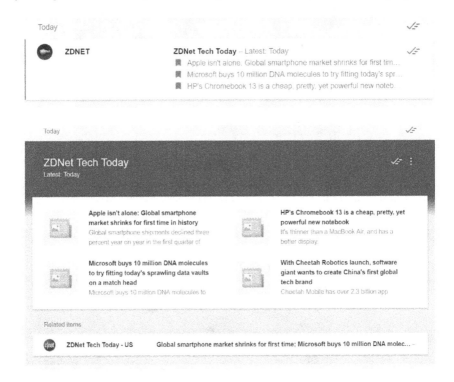

Newsletter Bundles will function similarly to Trips. As more emails related to the newsletter come in, they are listed below the main Newsletter card. At the time of this writing, not too many Newsletters are included, but more will be added as quickly as possible.

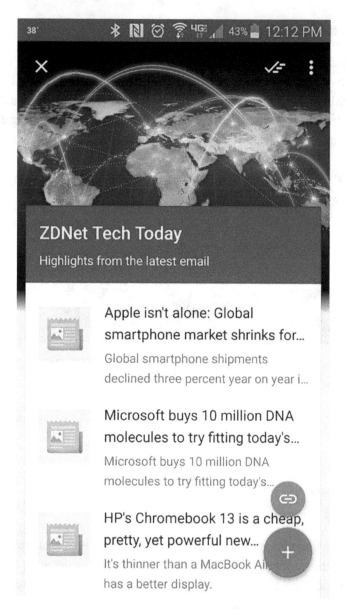

You cannot turn off this capability, however, there is an option to unbundle each on an individual basis. These also do not have the ability to schedule when they appear as with other bundles.

Events Bundle

Events Bundles are also similar to Trips as they will aggregate all the emails related to a specific event. If you have an Event Bundle, you will see a calendar icon in the Inbox with the event name, date, time and location. As emails are automatically added to the bundle, the summary will display the detail(s) that have changed. You can then expand the bundle to see the complete history of the event as well as all of the emails associated with that event.

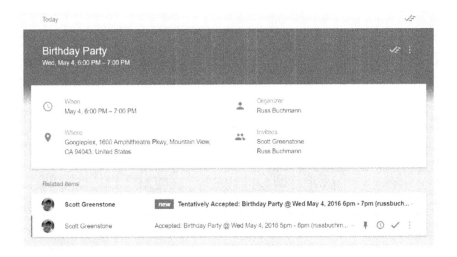

Similar to Trips and Newsletters, you will be able to delete these events without deleting the emails themselves. You will not have the ability to schedule when they appear as with other bundles. But, that should not be an issue since they are most likely scheduled in your calendar anyway.

13

Save to Inbox

Save to Inbox allows users to save links from apps, websites, and clipboard history directly to Inbox by Gmail. Using the mobile version (iOS and Android) when users click on the share option, there will be a new option, Save to Inbox, in the sharing menu. When using your desktop computer, a new extension has been rolled out for Chrome that provides this functionality. The extension can be found by going here:

https://chrome.google.com/webstore/detail/inbox-by-gmail/gkljgfmjocfalijkgoogmfffkhmkbgol.

You will only have the option to share at the time you use the extension. Once saved in Inbox, there is no share capability. In addition, if you don't click on the extension to Save to Inbox and instead manually copy a URL or Link, when you go back to Inbox there will be a new Link icon above the Floating Action Button (FAB) that will give you an option to share that newly copied link.

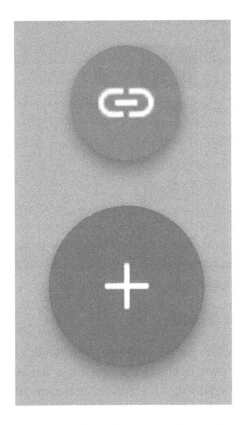

The benefit for this feature will be the automatic creation of a new Bundle named "Saved" which will keep all of these links grouped together. For example, if you come across news articles that you don't have time to read, you can save them to Inbox and show the bundle as they arrive. It could be once a day or once a week depending on your needs. You can also get more granular and snooze individual saved links to appear at the time you want to see them.

The Saved Bundle will default to show messages as they arrive (meaning at the time you save the link). You can always change this from the settings menu or the gear icon next to that bundle.

User Generated Bundles

Here is where you can really customize your Inbox organization. If you have created your own labels in classic Gmail, these will automatically transfer to Inbox by Gmail. As a default, these are NOT bundled in the inbox. So if they are important and you need to know when new messages arrive in these bundles, I suggest changing that setting. You will see why a little bit later.

Creating/Deleting/Editing a new label is much simpler in Inbox than it is in classic Gmail:

1. Click on the create new menu item.

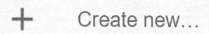

2. On the next screen, you can add your filters and choose to either edit or delete the bundle.

16

Settings

Automatically add messages

ADD

Edit name   Delete

3. When you click "add", you will be able to enter the specifics of what messages you want to go into the bundle. Using the drop down menu, you can choose "From", "To", "Subject", or base it on whether an email includes or excludes certain words. You can add as much as you want and be as specific as you want. Use a comma to separate the "from" or "to" addresses. Most advanced search (https://support.google.com/mail/answer/7190?hl=en) features found in Gmail will work in these fields as well.

4. These new filters will only apply to future messages. They will not apply to existing ones in Inbox.

Automatically add messages

From   ▾   Name or email

And...   ▾

Will apply to future messages like the ones below.   CANCEL   SAVE

In a similar manner to classic Gmail, if you remove a label or bundle, it will not delete the emails in that bundle. It will just remove the label from the message.

Removing from Bundle

Sometimes you may have automatically (or manually) added an email to a bundle by mistake. Thankfully, Inbox includes the capability to remove an email from a bundle. This process, however, will remove the entire conversation. It will not remove just a single message from the conversation.

To remove an email from a bundle, simply open the email, click the three dots to the right of the email subject line, and choose Remove from [Bundle Name].

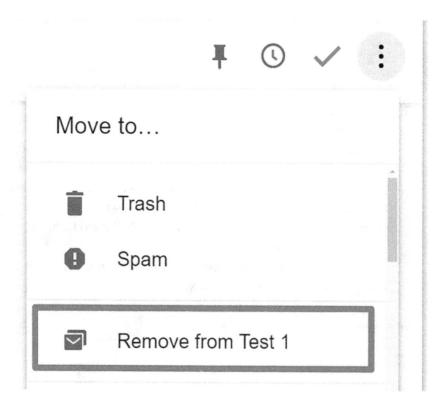

Adding Emails to a Bundle

Every now and then, an email comes into your inbox that has not been previously assigned to a bundle. Inbox provides a mechanism to not only add this particular email to a bundle, but will also give you the option to continue adding emails from this sender to that bundle.

Click on the three dots to the right of the subject line and choose Move to [Bundle Name]. You will then see a message on the bottom left of the screen offering "Undo" and "Always Do" this. If you choose "Always Do" this, Inbox will add this email to the Bundling criteria in the bundle settings.

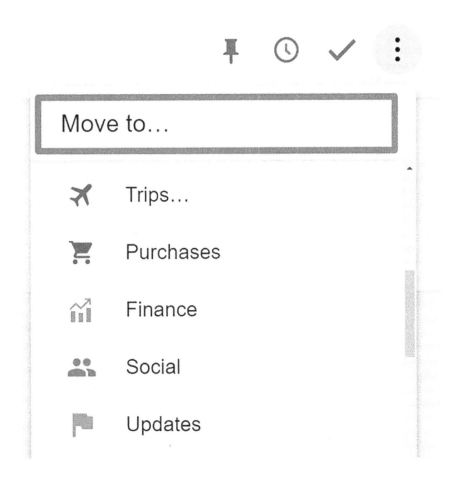

Show Original

Similar to classic Gmail, Inbox offers users the ability to Show Original, which essentially gives users the capability to view the email headers. You can view the headers by clicking on the overflow menu of the individual (not entire thread) email and choose Show Original, and you can see headers similar to those shown below.

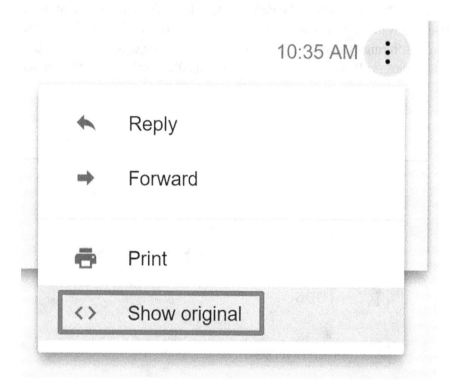

This feature will greatly assist users with troubleshooting any delivery issues that may be experienced such as delays and fake email addresses known as "spoofing". Below is a sample of only a portion of the information provided by using "Show Original" to give you an idea of what it looks like. It may be technical gibberish to most, but it can provide valuable information to those who understand how to read and interpret the routing information it provides.

```
Delivered-To:        ███              .com
Received: by       ███  ███ with SMTP id u143csp1055301vke;
        Mon, 2 May 2016 07:35:06 -0700 (PDT)
X-Received: by 10.129.153.68 with SMTP id q65mr18306142ywg.135.
        Mon, 02 May 2016 07:35:06 -0700 (PDT)
Return-Path: <_ ███ ███████  ███@gmail.com>
Received: from mail-yw0-x22b.google.com (mail-yw0-x22b.google.cc
        by mx.google.com with ESMTPS id u75si8005377ywu.352.201(
        for < ███ ███ ███ ██ ¨.com>
        (version=TLS1_2 cipher=ECDHE-RSA-AES128-GCM-SHA256 bits
        Mon, 02 May 2016 07:35:06 -0700 (PDT)
Received-SPF: pass (google.com: domain of        ██ @gmai
client-ip=2607:f8b0:4002:c05::22b;
Authentication-Results: mx.google.com;
        dkim=pass header.i=@gmail.com;
        spf=pass (google.com: domain of ████████  █████@gmail.c
smtp.mailfrom=████  █████  @gmail.com;
        dmarc=pass (p=NONE dis=NONE) header.from=gmail.com
Received: by mail-yw0-x22b.google.com with SMTP id o66so2882310;
        for <█████  █████  .com>; Mon, 02 May 2016 07:35:06
DKIM-Signature: v=1; a=rsa-sha256; c=relaxed/relaxed;
        d=gmail.com; s=20120113;
        h=mime-version:references:in-reply-to:from:date:message
        bh=XujEnds+MFLlXUKxF7/0e7nKN+C74hZalO01Ga1rAwA=;
        b=tEAli5Noxsr4AFOD6aUMIootAryB7bAJS/tshhTxts3XBRbHhpzw4l
         LVlwJ5X/vnowVl2wrig8+VcZzba3Xab0KP0x5LzyP/zZUonarIYaUo(
         L4MoUpIkphmhixIndZ0icDDxy+Ur1UcijFG2Ym6BRX0i7lR541Ww4Z
         ZZOzQevKSbD+Uki/TM6j0k7vdahfGdENCYLScx2r46bJ1pBIaG/l+8'
```

Done? Are We Ever Done?

Inbox offers a unique workflow from current email programs, and as part of this workflow, the terminology is unique as well. Unlike every other email program out there, Inbox does not have Mark as Un/Read or Archive. Instead, they offer the ability to Done your emails.

When you mark an email as Done in Inbox, you are essentially telling the system you no longer need this message in your Inbox. Inbox helps minimize your work effort by allowing you to mark an email as Done without even opening the message, thus negating the need to mark as read. So when you mark the email as Done, it leaves your Inbox and gets reassigned to the Done bundle. Yes, the message is still bold and unread, but who cares? The bundles do not show an unread count, so it is out of your way. In addition to marking individual emails as Done, Inbox offers users the opportunity to Sweep a bunch of emails at once. So once you are done snoozing, deleting, pinning, or reading, you can click the Sweep (✔=) icon to mark all emails from that section that are not pinned as Done. This will remove all of them from the inbox and place them in the Done bundle. You can always get to them again by viewing the Done bundle or any other bundle to which they were assigned.

What to do when Done with your message

There are essentially two things you can do in Inbox when you are Done with a message. You can move the item to the Done bundle, or you can move the message directly to the Trash. Inbox offers you a nice option in the settings menu where you can select what you prefer to have done when removing messages. If you select Mark as Done, then the status quo will remain and all menus and icons will stay the same. But if you choose Move to Trash, then the Done check mark changes to a Trash icon, and the Move To menu item for Trash changes to Done.

Settings

Labels

Signature

Snooze

Other

☑ Keyboard shortcuts
Tip: Hit "Shift + ?" to see the keyboard shortcuts

☐ Redirect Gmail to inbox.google.com
Always take me to Inbox when I visit Gmail in a web
browser. You can always get back to Gmail by clicking on
the link in the main menu.

☐ Make notifications stay on the screen longer
Notifications will stay on screen for 30 seconds

When removing messages, I prefer to...

◉ Mark as Done

○ Move to Trash

DONE

23

Snoozing for Later

Sometimes, you get emails you know you don't need to deal with now. But before Inbox, what would you do with them? If you moved them to another folder, how would you know if you needed to act on them again? With Inbox, you have one of the greatest features in email management - Snooze. Snoozing lets you get the email out of sight and brings it back at a time or place that you indicate. Simple as that. This is one of the features I use most to help me get to Inbox Zero throughout the day.

As Inbox has developed, so has the capabilities and intuitiveness of Snoozing. Inbox provides users with the ability to customize the default snooze times for Morning, Afternoon and Evening and will sync across all of your devices using Inbox. With travel reservations, you will now be presented with an option to snooze to the day before the trip. For shipping confirmations, it allows you to snooze to the scheduled date of delivery.

In addition to the system generated snooze times, Inbox lets you snooze an email to reappear at specific times or a specific location. So if you are using the mobile Inbox app and are near a specific location, emails snoozed to that location will reappear in your Inbox and provide a notification (assuming notifications are turned on for your device).

Snoozing by Time

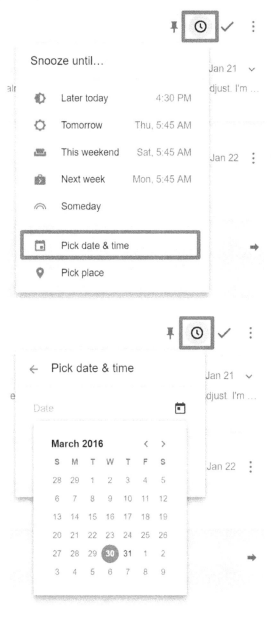

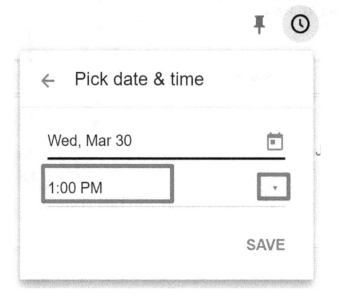

Snoozing by Place

Here you will be given the options that have already been saved during previous snooze to place selections, as well as your home and work locations if you have them set in Google Maps. Or, you can just enter a new location in the Enter Address field.

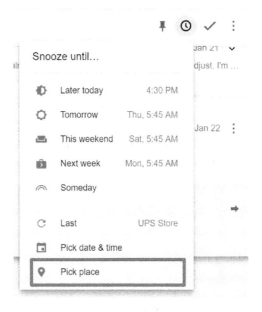

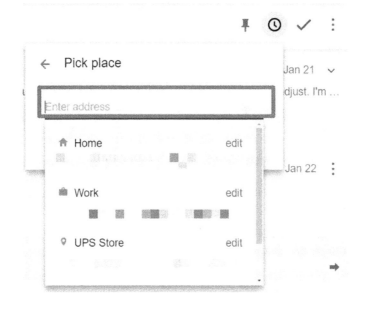

Pinning

Inbox provides users with the ability to keep emails that they want to follow up on but don't necessarily want to Snooze them out of sight. Clicking on the Pin icon ✝ in the Inbox will keep the email in the Inbox for future reference. By using the Pin feature while viewing bundles, you can quickly move the email back to the Inbox. Emails that are Pinned are not affected by the sweep action and thus remain in the Inbox.

When in the Inbox you also have the option to see only those emails that are Pinned by clicking on the Pin slider at the top.

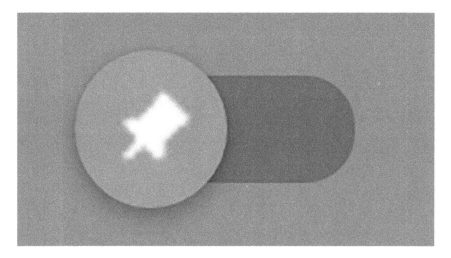

Essentially, there are three reasons to Pin an email:

1. Move bundled emails back to the inbox.
2. Move done or snoozed emails back to the inbox.
3. Perform sweep actions on all unpinned emails in the inbox in one click.

Trash

Similar to classic Gmail, Inbox provides the ability to delete emails and will keep them for you for 30 days. By moving an email to trash, you are deleting the email. However, you will have 30 days to essentially change your mind.

Inside the Trash bundle, you are able to remove the message from trash so you do not lose it. But, you can also empty the trash if you would like. To remove a message from trash, just select the email by clicking on the avatar to change it to a check mark. Then you will see options at the top that will let you Pin the trashed item back to the Inbox, Snooze it, Mark it as Done, or move it to another location by clicking the three vertical dots.

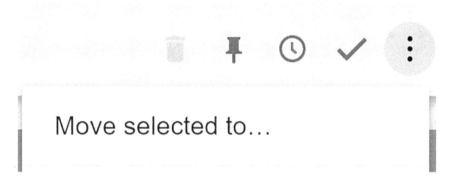

You cannot permanently delete one email at a time; you can only permanently delete the entire trash bundle.

Items that have been in Trash more than 30 days will be automatically deleted.

EMPTY TRASH NOW

Spam

Google has powerful tools employed behind the scenes to identify emails that are junk or spam. Ones that most of the time we don't even want to see, or they could be potentially harmful if we opened them and clicked on a link inside the message. As a result, all of these messages end up in the

Spam folder. It is important to periodically check your spam bundle, as sometimes, messages that we want in our Inbox get miscategorized as Spam.

Here are the steps for removing email from Spam:

1. Go to *inbox.google.com*.
2. Click on the menu drop down icon ▤.
3. Select the Spam bundle.
4. Open the email that you feel is classified incorrectly.
5. Pin the email back to your Inbox by clicking on the Pin 📌.
6. If you have a lot of emails in your inbox, you can quickly find all of those pinned to the inbox by using the pin slider icon at the top of the screen ⬤.
7. Refreshing the page will reactivate any links deactivated by the spam checker.

Messages in the Spam label will automatically delete after 30 days, however, you can empty the spam manually by selecting the Empty Spam Now link at the top of the Spam label.

Items that have been in Spam more than 30 days will be automatically deleted.

EMPTY SPAM NOW

Reminders Are Your Tasks

Tasks in Gmail have been a widely used feature. I personally have not taken to Gmail Tasks due to various reasons. Mostly I have not been a fan of tasks because, really, what good is a task without a reminder?

With the introduction of Inbox by Gmail, there have been a great deal of inquiries, and complaints for that matter, regarding Task implementation in Inbox. My usual answer to them has been that short of migrating existing tasks into Inbox, tasks already exist in Inbox with Reminders.

There are multiple ways of creating reminders in the Google ecosystem including Inbox, Keep Calendar, and Google Now.

Inbox Reminders take Tasks to an entirely new level by bringing the task back to your attention at either a specific time or location, and it can do this once or on a repeating schedule. Reminders in Inbox take it even one step further by providing suggestions as you enter your reminder. Type in Call Mom, and mom's phone number will be added to the reminder. Type in a reminder to purchase something at a specific store, and the open or closed status may appear. With some more common reminders, Inbox will automatically add an identifying icon such as a phone for calls or a calendar icon for something like paying taxes. Some emails that even mention a task to do in the text will present you with an option to create a reminder for that email and task. Below are some examples of what these reminders may look like. Read more on this in the section below entitled Assists.

In addition to standalone reminders, Inbox allows you to create reminders associated with a specific email. The snoozing and assist functionalities work the same here as with the standalone reminders. To create a reminder associated with an email, you first need to snooze the email or pin the email and then the reminder option will appear.

What is nice with these reminders is they will display on the Google Calendar App and on the Android Google Calendar Widget.

Contacts

Unlike classic Gmail, Inbox does not have the ability to add contacts directly from an email; contacts need to be added using the contacts page at *contacts.google.com*. This page can also be accessed directly from the left side menu by clicking on the word contacts.

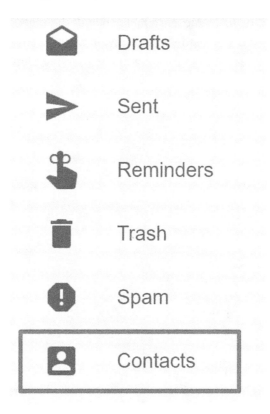

Inbox currently does not have the ability to email Groups created in Contacts. It is widely hoped that this feature is added sometime in the future.

Keyboard Shortcuts

As with classic Gmail, Inbox by Gmail offers users the ability to use keyboard shortcuts to perform common actions much quicker. In order to use keyboard shortcuts, users must make sure that these are turned on in settings under the other sections. Unlike classic Gmail, Inbox does not provide the ability to create custom keyboard shortcuts. See the image below for all of the keyboard shortcuts available in Inbox by Gmail. This list can also be accessed from the program by pressing Shift+?.

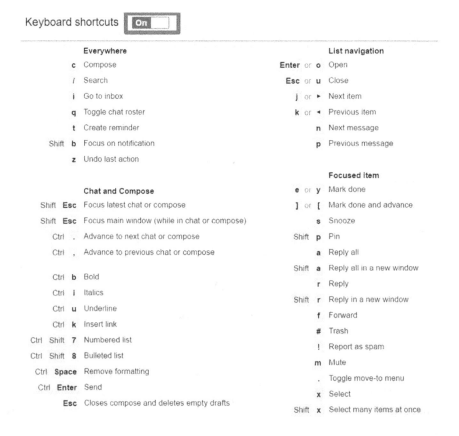

Keyboard shortcuts **On**

Everywhere		
c	Compose	
/	Search	
i	Go to inbox	
q	Toggle chat roster	
t	Create reminder	
Shift b	Focus on notification	
z	Undo last action	

Chat and Compose		
Shift Esc	Focus latest chat or compose
Shift Esc	Focus main window (while in chat or compose)
Ctrl .	Advance to next chat or compose
Ctrl ,	Advance to previous chat or compose
Ctrl b	Bold
Ctrl i	Italics
Ctrl u	Underline
Ctrl k	Insert link
Ctrl Shift 7	Numbered list
Ctrl Shift 8	Bulleted list
Ctrl Space	Remove formatting
Ctrl Enter	Send
Esc	Closes compose and deletes empty drafts

List navigation		
Enter or o	Open
Esc or u	Close
j or ►	Next item
k or ◄	Previous item
n	Next message
p	Previous message

Focused item		
e or y	Mark done
] or [	Mark done and advance
s	Snooze
Shift p	Pin
a	Reply all
Shift a	Reply all in a new window
r	Reply
Shift r	Reply in a new window
f	Forward
#	Trash
!	Report as spam
m	Mute
.	Toggle move-to menu
x	Select
Shift x	Select many items at once

Available Settings

Inbox is a very minimalistic program that utilizes many of the settings from classic Gmail. As a result, there are only a few modifications that can be made using Inbox. More detailed settings and changes can be made from the Gmail settings page which will be reflected in Inbox by Gmail. Inbox offers Label settings, Signature Settings, Snooze Settings and Other settings. All of these are discussed elsewhere in this book.

Settings

Labels

Signature

Snooze

Other

Labels

The label settings are a way to quickly access the settings for each bundle. It is just like you would be able to by using the gear icon next to the Bundle name in the menu list. Here you have a quick toggle for each Bundle to let Inbox know if you want to bundle these messages in the Inbox. You can also see a quick indication of any inbox bundling limitations such as once a day or once a week. If there is no indication, then the messages will bundle in the inbox as they arrive.

In addition to the quick information and toggle, you have your standard settings gear icon to bring you to the full settings window of that bundle. It includes the criteria for automatically adding messages, the ability to add more criteria, as well as the inbox bundling settings and timing. From here you can also change the name of the bundle as well as completely delete the bundle. Deleting the bundle will not delete the emails that are in that bundle, it will only remove that bundle assignment to that email.

Signature

Inbox allows users to set up a basic signature that will append to your messages when sent. These are simple text signatures. If you want a bit more formatting, like hyperlinks or color, you can create those in another text editor, and then copy and paste them into the signature settings for Inbox. You will not see these signatures while you are composing your email, rather they get added to the email at the time you send.

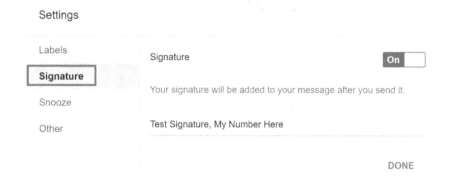

Snooze

The snooze settings allow users to specify what time each daypart is associated with and individually customize the snooze experience. As long as they are sequential, you can specify any time you want for Morning, Afternoon, or Evening.

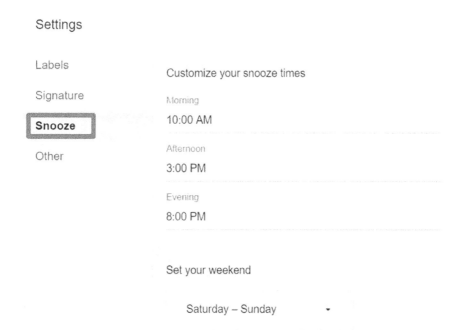

Settings

Labels

Signature

Snooze

Other

Customize your snooze times

Morning

10:00 AM

Afternoon

3:00 PM

Evening

8:00 PM

Set your weekend

Saturday – Sunday   ▾

Other

Other settings are somewhat of a catchall for any other settings that cannot be categorized. It is where you will be able to turn the Keyboard Shortcuts on or off and lengthen the amount of time notifications stay on the screen. You can select your preferential action when removing a message by choosing "Mark as Done" or "Move to Trash".

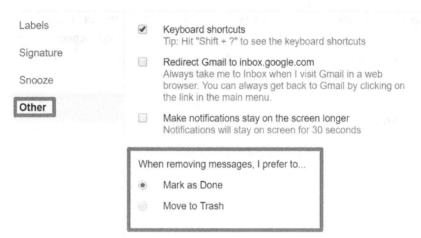

Settings

Labels

Signature

Snooze

Other

☑ Keyboard shortcuts
Tip: Hit "Shift + ?" to see the keyboard shortcuts

☐ Redirect Gmail to inbox.google.com
Always take me to Inbox when I visit Gmail in a web browser. You can always get back to Gmail by clicking on the link in the main menu.

☐ Make notifications stay on the screen longer
Notifications will stay on screen for 30 seconds

When removing messages, I prefer to...

◉ Mark as Done

◌ Move to Trash

DONE

In addition to those three settings, the Inbox team added a nice feature to help you get to Inbox quickly. On Google.com and inside the Google Launcher you have links/icons that will bring you directly to Gmail. They provided the option to automatically redirect Gmail URLs to inbox.google.com. So whenever you click a Gmail link, you will be brought to Inbox. If you toggle this option on, a new item will be listed in the left side menu that will bring you to Gmail if necessary. This setting will not impact the mail handler in Chrome. If you have that set for Gmail, clicking on email links or addresses will still open up in Gmail.

Assists

Inbox is all about efficiency and taking the least amount of time to accomplish the task at hand. No feature in Inbox demonstrates this more than Assists. Simply put, Assists are 20[6] different bits of information that help take you through the rest of the task at hand. Essentially, Inbox knows what you entered in your reminder and provides you with the next piece of information such as the phone number, address, email address or other piece of information. Assists will provide you with open hours for a business, help you assign a doctor/dentist so their contact info is included, or even provide you with the number of days left until an event mentioned in the reminder.

You will see the assist show up in the reminders bundle, and you can click on the blue question to populate the information. Next time you create a reminder or snooze to a location and say dentist, that information will appear automatically.

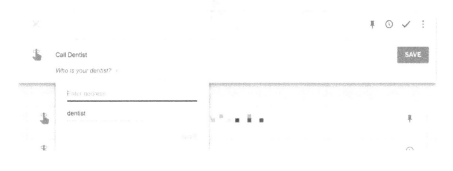

---

6   http://gmailblog.blogspot.com/2014/12/assists-in-inbox-extra-helping-hand-for.html

Answer Cards

Answer cards are an easy way to find important information that may be buried somewhere in your Inbox whether it is bundled or just under the Done label. By just searching for coupon codes, frequent flyer account numbers, or usernames that may be inside an email, Inbox will prominently display the relevant information as well as a list of emails that may have matched that search.

Highlights

Inbox also makes finding embedded information in your emails easier by "highlighting" that information. Time is saved by not having to open the email and locate the information. As of this writing, Inbox highlights flight reservations, order information, package tracking, hotel reservations, restaurant reservations, ticketed events, bills, news and other articles. [7]

---

[7] https://developers.google.com/gmail/markup/highlights

Searching

Searching is by far the fastest and most efficient way to find your emails. The benefit of searching over labeling is there is no need to remember what label a message is in. So as a result, you can just put search criteria in the search field, and your results will have exactly what you are looking for.

Results are broken down into two sections: Top results and All results. The top results include the top messages that Google decides are the most relevant to your search criteria.

Search is the foundation of Google, and its capabilities were definitely included in Inbox by Gmail. Most of the search criteria and capabilities found in Gmail have been transferred over to Inbox including the advanced search features. You can search using "in:", "from:", "to:", "subject:" and exclusions using the minus sign, etc. All of the advanced search criteria can be found in the Gmail Support pages[8].

Because of the advanced search capabilities, I was able to completely

---

[8] https://support.google.com/mail/answer/7190?hl=en

abandon labels in Inbox. I was able to remove approximately 60 labels and sub-labels, and now I use labels exclusively for testing purposes when supporting users in the help forums.

Mobile

It is not uncommon for web-based software to offer a Mobile version. Usually, however, the execution of the Mobile application is drastically different from the web version. This goes for the user interface as well as features, settings, and options.

In contrast, Inbox seems to have broken this mold with regards to email programs. They have not only developed an intuitive, easy-to-use web interface, but they also successfully replicated this on the mobile platform. Any changes you make in one instance of Inbox are nicely reflected in the other.

Smart Replies

Inbox makes the task of responding to emails just a little bit easier with Smart Replies. Users will be prompted with up to three possible "quick replies" based on the email they are replying to. They will have the option of selecting one of the smart replies or responding in the way you normally would have. What is nice is that you can choose one of the smart replies and then add more to make the reply more personal or more detailed.

There should be no concern over privacy. Smart Replies are all based on algorithmic data, and nobody is reading your emails. Machine learning is used to improve future suggestions based on responses you select over time. You can also be comfortable in knowing that the suggestions that are provided will be suitable for work situations.

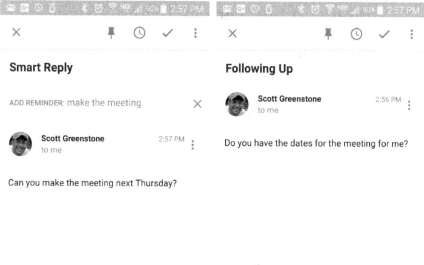

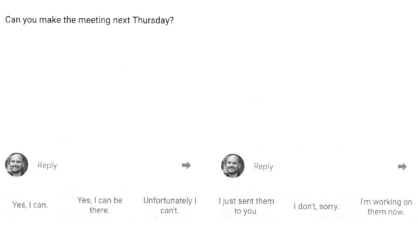

Bonus: Inbox Zero in 3 Simple Steps

It seems that every day I see an article, post, or tweet about how one can reach Inbox Zero. Well now it's my turn, and I do it every day (even multiple times throughout the day) using three simple steps. Using classic Gmail, I have never been able to reach Inbox Zero. Interestingly, ever since Inbox by Gmail came along I am able to successfully reach this lofty goal multiple times EVERY SINGLE DAY.

It took some time to get my Inbox settings just right in order to allow me to accomplish this quickly and easily. Many people use and refer to a formal efficiency process called "GTD", or "Getting Things Done". Nevertheless, I am a simple man and need less formality to reach my goals. I have read GTD as it pertains to email, and it includes obvious steps: don't spend more than 2 minutes per email and then essentially file the email as "to do", "wait", or "follow up".

As I just mentioned, my technique is a bit less formal. But before we get to my process (which honestly will sound pretty obvious once you read it), we should review my Inbox by Gmail setup. When I switched to Inbox by Gmail, I abandoned all of my existing labels in classic Gmail. Thanks to some very effective convincing by some friends, not only did I stop using all my labels (which had multiple sub labels), but I completely deleted all of my labels. I rely 100% on the incredible strength of the search function in Inbox by Gmail, and I have never had difficulty finding the emails I need. Currently, I am left with only the system generated bundles - most of which I have set to bundle in the inbox as emails arrive. I have one or two bundles set to bundle in the inbox "Once a Day at 7:00 AM". I will most likely change this setting for other bundles if Inbox ever adds custom bundling times. For me, 7:00 AM is not a great time to see a ton of emails come in.

Now here is what I have been doing consistently to reach Inbox Zero multiple times throughout each day.

Step 1: Reply

This is the first step in cleaning out my inbox. I quickly scan through my new messages. With Inbox by Gmail, I can quickly determine whether or not I need to reply to an email just by seeing the subject and who it is from. If it is one that I need to reply to, I draft the reply and send it off. I don't do anything further other than close the email and it remains in the inbox for me to tend to later in my process.

Step 2: Snooze

Snoozing is the greatest feature, in my opinion, that Inbox by Gmail offers. When employed properly, snoozing can be your best tool for reaching inbox zero. As I am scanning through my emails as noted in Step 1, I can quickly identify emails that I can "put away" for later, or "snooze". For example, I get reminder emails for bills I have coming up. They usually arrive anywhere from 15 days to 1 month before the bill is due. I pay my upcoming bills on Sunday, so I snooze all bill reminders to the Sunday Evening that is at least 1 week prior to the bill's due date. If I have a project where I need to send something out to someone else, I will snooze the email until 2 days prior to when I need to send that email. That way it gives me ample time to remember to work on that item before I need to send it out. Another example includes notifications that tell me I have mail at my UPS Store mailbox. I snooze these to a location, rather than time, so it reappears when I am close to my UPS Store.

Snooze until…

☼	Tomorrow	Thu, 5:45 AM
🛋	This weekend	Sat, 5:45 AM
💼	Next week	Mon, 5:45 AM
◠	Someday	

📅	Pick date & time
📍	Pick place

Step 3: Sweep to Done

So Steps 1 and 2 have essentially completed my email work for that session. Since I have scanned through all of my emails to determine which ones qualify for Step 1 or 2, the remainder is usually junk or emails that I just needed to read and not act on. All that is left in my inbox after Step 1 and 2 are emails that I already acted upon and emails that require no action by me. Now all I need to do is "Sweep to Done" all the remaining emails.

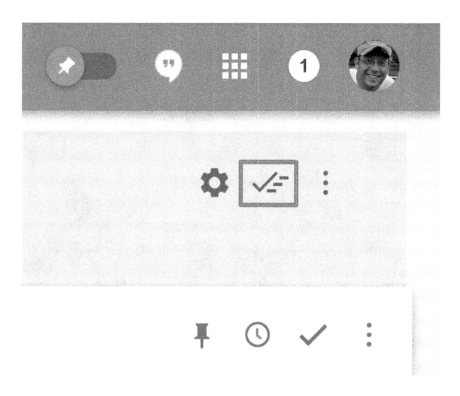

And there you have it - Inbox Zero. It's efficient, simple and effective. This is how it works for me. It may not work for everyone out there, but it is simple enough to give it a try.

Appendix

Google Top Contributor Program? What's that?

Google Product Forums are a place where people come to get support on issues they are experiencing with the products. Google has so many users of their free products that it is impossible for them to provide live customer service via chat, email or phone. Enter the Google Product forums. Google needs a way that is cost effective to provide support through these product forums. In an ingenious fashion, they have taken to its user base to obtain volunteer "support staff." This is done through the Google Top Contributor Program (https://topcontributor.withgoogle.com/).

To quote Google:

> ## *"Top Contributors share their Google knowledge to help the world thrive online.*
>
> *Top Contributors are the lifeblood of Google Help Forums and the wider Google community. Passionate about Google products, they help millions of people around the world."*

The Top Contributor Program is somewhat exclusive in that you need to be invited to join. First you are assigned the title of "Rising Star". Eventually, if the quantity and quality of your responses meet certain criteria, you get invited to be a "Top Contributor". Once you become a Top Contributor you get access to a lot of perks.

Participation in this program has proven to be highly rewarding. Not only for the satisfaction of all the thousands of users we help, but also because of the friends you make from all over the world. The Top Contributor Program is actually how Russ and I (virtually) met. We have developed such a great friendship that we teamed up to bring you this, our first book. Our friendship, and others that we have made through the program, will be lasting and very meaningful.

www.ingramcontent.com/pod-product-compliance
Lightning Source LLC
Chambersburg PA
CBHW061052050326
40690CB00012B/2594